I WONDER WHY

The Wind Blows

KINGFISHER
LONDON & NEW YORK

KINGFISHER
LONDON & NEW YORK

Copyright © Macmillan Publishers
International Ltd 2011, 2024
Published in the United States by Kingfisher
120 Broadway, New York, NY 10271
Kingfisher is a division of Macmillan
Children's Books, London

ISBN: 978-0-7534-7928-5 (HB)
ISBN: 978-0-7534-7927-8 (PB)

Distributed in the U.S. and Canada by Macmillan,
120 Broadway, New York, NY 10271

EU representative: Macmillan Publishers Ireland Ltd,
1st Floor, The Liffey Trust Centre,
117-126 Sheriff Street Upper, Dublin 1, D01 YC43.

Library of Congress Cataloging-in-Publication
data has been applied for.

Author: Anita Ganeri

2024 edition
Editor: Seeta Parmar
Designers: Peter Clayman, Amelia Brooks
Illustrator: Marie-Eve Tremblay

Kingfisher books are available for special
promotions and premiums. For details contact:
Special Markets Department, Macmillan,
120 Broadway, New York, NY 10271.

For more information, please visit
www.kingfisherbooks.com.

Printed in China
9 8 7 6 5 4 3 2 1
1TR/1123/WKT/RV/128MA

FSC
www.fsc.org

MIX
Paper | Supporting
responsible forestry
FSC® C116313

CONTENTS

Is Earth round?

If you were an astronaut floating about in space, Earth would look like a **gigantic ball**. It isn't perfectly round, though. Like a ball that's been **gently squashed**, it's slightly flatter at the top and bottom, and it bulges out just a little in the middle.

Earth measures 24,900 miles (40,075km) around its "waist"—the equator. If you walked night and day, it would take you more than a year to travel that distance!

EQUATOR

Earth looks blue from space. That's because almost three-fourths of it is covered by water.

It's very hot at the center of Earth—more than 9,000°F (5,000°C). For comparison, a really hot summer's day can be 85–100°F (30–40°C).

CRUST

The crust is the rocky layer beneath your feet.

MANTLE

The mantle is a thick layer of rock. It's so hot that some of the rock has melted.

The core is made of metal. The outer core is runny and liquid, but the inner core is solid.

OUTER CORE

INNER CORE

What is Earth made of?

Earth is made up of different layers of **rock and metal**. Some of the layers are hard, but others are so hot that they've melted and are runny—a little like hot, sticky caramel.

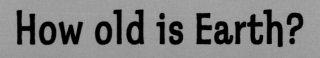

How old is Earth?

Scientists think Earth formed about **4,600 million years ago**—although no one was there to see it! They think the Moon formed then, too.

About 200 million years ago there was just one super-continent called Pangaea.

PANGAEA

About 180 million years ago Pangaea began to break up.

Modern human beings are very new to Earth. If you imagine our planet's 4.6-billion-year history squeezed into one year, people have been around only since late on December 31!

Continents are massive pieces of land. There are seven of them in all. Trace them from a map, and try to see how they once fitted together.

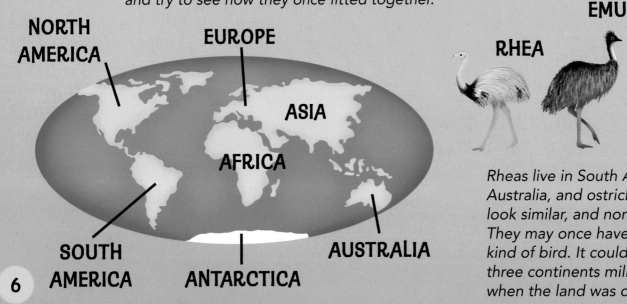

NORTH AMERICA

EUROPE

ASIA

AFRICA

SOUTH AMERICA

ANTARCTICA

AUSTRALIA

RHEA

EMU

OSTRICH

Rheas live in South America, emus in Australia, and ostriches in Africa. They look similar, and none of them can fly. They may once have been related to one kind of bird. It could have walked to all three continents millions of years ago, when the land was connected.

Has Earth changed much?

Yes, it has! About 200 million years ago, most of the land was **joined together** in one big piece. Then it began to break up into smaller pieces called continents. These slowly **drifted apart**, until they reached the places they're in today.

About 66 million years ago the continents drifted farther apart.

Today, the continents are still drifting.

North America and Europe are still moving apart by about 1.5 inches (4cm) each year. That's about the length of your thumb.

Where are the highest mountains?

The Himalayas in Asia are the world's highest mountains. They're so high that they're known as **"the roof of the world."** The towering mountain peaks are bitterly cold places, where the snow and ice never melt.

These are the highest mountains in each continent:

Asia—Mt. Everest 29,032 ft. (8,849m)

South America—Aconcagua 22,837 ft. (6,961m)

North America—Denali 20,310 ft. (6,190m)

Africa—Mt. Kilimanjaro 19,341 ft. (5,895m)

Europe —Mt. Elbrus 18,510 ft. (5,642m)

Antarctica—Vinson Massif 16,050 ft. (4,892m)

Australia — Mt Kosciuszko 7,310 ft. (2,228m)

Himalaya means "home of the snows." It's a good name for these freezing peaks.

8

Can mountains shrink?

Many mountains are getting smaller all the time. Every day, small chips of rock are carried away by ice, snow, and running water. Some **mountains are getting bigger**, though. The Himalayas are still being pushed up by movements inside Earth.

In Hawaii, there is a mountain called Mauna Kea that is 4,265 feet (1,300m) taller than Mount Everest. Most of it is under the sea, though.

The higher you go up a mountain, the colder it becomes. Many of the animals that live up on mountains have thick, woolly coats to keep out the cold —goats, llamas, and yaks, for example.

Which mountains breathe fire?

Volcanoes are mountains that sometimes spurt out burning ash, gas, and hot, runny rock called **lava**. The gas and fiery lava come from deep down inside Earth, and burst up through **cracks in the crust**. Some volcanoes are active, meaning that they have recently erupted and will erupt again. Others are dormant, meaning they haven't erupted in a long time, or extinct, meaning they will not erupt in the future.

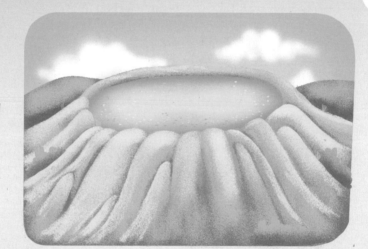

The saucerlike top of a volcano is called a crater. Sometimes a dead volcano's crater fills with rainwater and makes a beautiful lake.

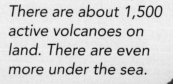

There are about 1,500 active volcanoes on land. There are even more under the sea.

The ash and dust from a volcano can get inside a plane's engines and damage them, leading to flights being canceled.

There are volcanoes in space, too. Olympus Mons on the planet Mars is three times higher than Earth's Mount Everest.

Do people live on volcanoes?

It's a risky thing to do, but many **people live on volcanoes**—especially farmers. The ash from a volcano makes the soil very rich, so the farmers can grow bumper crops.

What makes Earth shake?

Earth's surface is made up of **huge pieces of hard rock** which drift on the hot, runny rock below. Sometimes these pieces **push and shove** against each other, causing Earth to shake. This is what happens during an earthquake.

The greatest danger in an earthquake is a building collapsing on top of you. If you are able to, shelter under a table.

Animals seem to feel the land moving long before we do. Dogs howl, snakes wriggle out of their holes, and chickens run for their lives!

Can people tell if an earthquake is coming?

Scientists who study earthquakes are called **seismologists**. Although they know where earthquakes are likely to happen, they usually can't say exactly when.

In the worst earthquakes the ground cracks open, streets sink, and buildings crumble to piles of rubble.

People have tried to design earthquake-proof buildings. Some of the latest ones are shaped like pyramids or cones.

What's the difference between stalactites and stalagmites?

Stalactites and **stalagmites** are both long and pointed, like icicles made of rock. The only difference between them is that while stalactites grow **down** from the roof of a cave, stalagmites grow **up** from the floor.

Don't sit and watch a stalactite grow. It can take more than 1,000 years to get less than half an inch (1cm) longer!

People who like to explore the secret world of underground tunnels and caves are called spelunkers.

Bats love the darkness of caves. They roost in them during the daytime, and they use them as nurseries for their pups.

Thousands of years ago people sheltered in caves. They painted pictures of bison and woolly mammoths on the walls.

What is the Room of Candles?

Deep down below the mountain slopes of eastern Italy is a magical cave known as the **Room of Candles**. It gets its name from the spikes of rock that grow up from the floor of the cave, like candles. They are really stalagmites, and they grow in small cups of rock which look like candle holders.

Like all underground caves, the Room of Candles was made by rainwater trickling down and eating away at the rock.

Where do rivers begin?

Rivers start as **tiny streams**. Some streams start where springs bubble out of the ground. Others form on mountains, when the tips of icy glaciers begin to melt. And some trickle out of lakes.

On some mountains, huge rivers of ice grind slowly downhill. These ice rivers are called glaciers.

1 Rain falls on the hills and sinks into the ground.

2 Water trickles up out of a spring.

3 The stream joins others, and becomes a fast-flowing river.

Why do old rivers flow so slowly?

4 The river reaches flatter land. It gets wider and flows more slowly.

At the bottom of a hill, the ground becomes flatter, slowing the river down. Instead of rushing downhill in a straight line, the river flows in big bends called **meanders**.

Where do rivers end?

Most rivers end their journey at the sea. The mouth of the river is where fresh river water mixes with the **salty water** of the sea.

The world's shortest river is the D River in Oregon. At just 120 feet (37m), it is only about as long as ten canoes.

Some rivers don't flow into the sea. They flow into lakes instead, or drain into the ground.

5 *A river sometimes cuts through one of its bends—leaving behind a curvy ox-bow lake.*

6 *At its mouth, the river may join the salty water of the sea.*

Birds love feeding at a river mouth. They pull out the worms that live in the gooey mud!

How high is the sky?

The sky is part of an **invisible skin** of air around Earth. This skin is called the **atmosphere**, and it reaches out into space for about 300 miles (500km). There's a very important gas called **oxygen** in the atmosphere—we all need to breathe oxygen to stay alive.

3 Above the planes is the ozone layer. This works a little like sunscreen, protecting us from the Sun's burning rays.

2 Planes fly in the next layer, high above the clouds where the skies are clear. The air is thinner here, and has less oxygen in it.

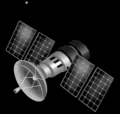

1 The atmosphere is made up of different layers. In the lowest layer, the air carries clouds and weather around Earth.

What is the greenhouse effect?

The greenhouse effect is the name scientists have given to a hot problem. **Waste gases** from factories, power plants, and cars are building up in the atmosphere and trapping too much heat close to Earth. Our planet is slowly **getting warmer**—like a greenhouse in summer.

If Earth gets too hot, the ice at the Poles could melt. The seas would rise and flood many towns along the coasts.

What are clouds made of?

Some clouds look like they're made of **cotton balls**—but they're not! Clouds are made of billions of **water droplets and ice crystals**. These are so tiny and light that they float in the air.

When does rain fall from clouds?

Rain falls when **water droplets** in a cloud start joining together. They get bigger and heavier until, in the end, they are too heavy to float, and fall to the ground as rain.

Without rain, no plants would grow. Then what would we all eat?

Have you ever heard of showers of frogs or fish? Well, they do happen! The animals are sometimes sucked up from ponds by extra strong winds. Later on, they fall to the ground with the rain.

You would need your umbrella on Mount Wai-'ale-'ale in Hawaii. It rains there for 350 days each year.

How cold is snow?

Snowflakes are water droplets that have frozen into **crystals of ice**. To stay frozen, they have to stay at freezing point—that's 32°F (0°C). If they get any warmer than that, snowflakes melt and fall to the ground as rain.

How big can you build a snowman? The tallest ever constructed was 122 feet (37m) high. That's about as tall as a eleven-story building.

Where do thunderstorms start?

Thunderstorms start in the **huge black thunderclouds** that sometimes gather at the end of a hot summer's day. Inside the clouds, strong winds hurl the water droplets around, and the cloud crackles with **electricity**. It flashes through the sky in great dazzling sparks, which we call lightning.

The biggest thunderclouds tower 10 miles (16km) into the air. That's almost twice the height of Mount Everest.

Lightning can travel as far as 87,000 miles (140,000km) in one second flat!

It's safest to stay inside during a thunderstorm. Never shelter under a tree— it might get struck by lightning.

What is thunder?

Sparks of lightning are **incredibly hot**. As they flash through the sky, they heat the air so quickly that it makes a **loud booming noise** like an explosion. This is thunder.

To find out how far away a storm is, count the number of seconds between the lightning and the thunder. The storm is one mile (1.6km) away for every five seconds you count.

1, 2, 3, 4, 5, 6.......

An American man was struck by lightning seven times! Roy C. Sullivan had his hair set alight twice and his eyebrows burnt off. He even lost a big toenail.

Why does the wind blow?

When you feel the wind blow, it's because air is on the move. Air moves when it's warm. It gets lighter and it rises up into the sky. **Cooler air** then rushes in to take its place, making a breeze.

Air is invisible, so you can't see the wind. But you can feel it on your face, and see how it makes the trees sway.

What is a tornado?

A tornado is a **spinning twist of wind** that speeds across the ground, sucking up everything in its path. Tornadoes happen mainly in North America. Hurricanes are another kind of spinning storm, but they begin over **warm tropical seas**. Hurricane winds can blow at speeds of up to 150 miles per hour (240km/h).

In Minnesota, in 1931, a tornado lifted a train into the air and dumped it in a ditch.

Where are rain forests?

The places where rain forests grow are shown below in green. These are the **world's warmest areas**, close to the equator.

Rain forests are home to over half of all the animals and plants that live on Earth.

EQUATOR

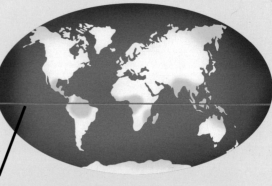

When does it rain in a rain forest?

It rains almost every day in a rain forest, but it doesn't pour all day long. The air gets **hotter and hotter**, and **stickier and stickier**, until there's a heavy thunderstorm in the afternoon. After that, it's dry again.

Anacondas are enormous snakes. They hide in the muddy waters of the Amazon, waiting for a tasty meal to pass by.

The world's biggest rain forest is in South America. It stretches for thousands of miles along the banks of the Amazon river.

Where is the biggest forest?

The world's biggest forest stretches across the top of Europe and Asia. The trees in this forest are **conifers**—they have hard, narrow leaves called needles.

BIGGEST FOREST

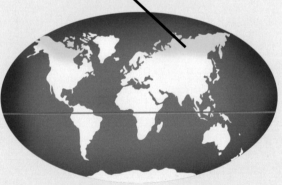

The conical shape of conifers and their drooping branches help snow slide off them.

Brown bears and wolves live in the dark forests of the north. Reindeer shelter there during the long cold winters.

27

Where does it never rain?

Deserts are the **driest places** in the world. In some deserts it never rains at all. In others, there isn't any rain for months or years on end. Deserts are very windy, too. The wind piles the sand up into big heaps, called **dunes**.

Many people who live in deserts are nomads. They move from place to place with their animals, looking for food and water.

Animals living in the desert have adapted to survive. Some live underground, and others get water from their food.

Which is the sandiest desert?

The Sahara Desert in North Africa is the biggest desert in the world. Huge parts of it are covered with **rolling hills of sand**. Desert land isn't always sandy, though. A lot of it is rocky, or covered with stones and gravel.

SAHARA DESERT

The Sahara Desert covers about one-third of the whole of Africa.

How hot are deserts?

In the hottest desert the temperature can rise to a **scorching 120°F (50°C)**, or more, and there no shade in sight. But then it cools down and gets really cold at night.

The Atacama Desert in Chile, South America, is the world's driest desert. For the past 500 years it experienced no rain. However, since 2015 there have been several heavy rainfalls.

What's it like at the poles?

Polar bears live at the North Pole, and penguins live at the South Pole. They never get the chance to meet!

The North and South Poles are at the very ends of the Earth. They are freezing-cold places with biting winds. **Ice and snow** stretch as far as the eye can see—not the best place for a vacation!

Antarctica is a huge ice-covered continent around the South Pole. In places, the ice is almost 3 miles (5km) thick.

Mount Erebus must be the warmest spot in Antarctica. It's an active volcano!

Which is the coldest place in the world?

MOUNT EREBUS

SOUTH POLE

VOSTOK STATION

Vostok Station is a really chilly spot in Antarctica. The temperature here is usually about –72°F (–58°C), but it has dropped to **–128°F (–89°C)**—the coldest ever known!

Where do polar bears live?

Polar bears live around the Arctic Ocean, near the North Pole. Funnily enough, they've never lived in Antarctica, though there's plenty of food and just as much snow and ice there.

Icebergs float in the sea. They were once part of rivers of ice called glaciers.

Polar bears never slip on the ice. The rough skin and hair on the soles of their feet give them a bit of extra grip.

INDEX